Gwathmey Siegel Apartments

Gwathmey Siegel & Associates Architects

Gwathmey Siegel Apartments

Preface
Charles Gwathmey

Introduction
Paul Goldberger

Edited by
Brad Collins

Gwathmey Siegel & Associates Architects

First published in the United States of America in 2004 by
RIZZOLI INTERNATIONAL PUBLICATIONS, INC.
300 Park Avenue South, New York, New York 10010
www.rizzoliusa.com

ISBN: 0-8478-2686-4
LCCN: 2004093147

outside cover: Miranova Penthouse, photography © Scott Frances/Esto
inside front flap: Central Park South Apartment, photography © Scott Frances/Esto

Design and type composition by group c inc / New Haven (BC, SC)
Printed and bound in Hong Kong

2004 2005 2006 2007 2008 / 10 9 8 7 6 5 4 3 2 1

Contents

Preface

I recently revisited LeCorbusier's Villa Savoye—which I first experienced in 1962—and realized that, without question, it was the initial, referential inspiration for my interest in designing apartments. The "free plan," the literal disassociation of the walls from the structure, creates the opportunity to explore composite plan and sectional manipulations that reinforce the formal strategy of object/frame.

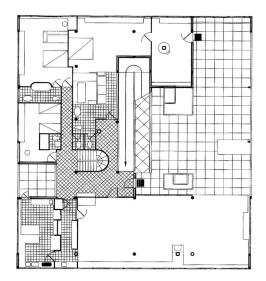

The design of apartments is, by our definition, an intervention—a series of formal, eccentric, often uniquely site-specific manipulations that accommodates and transforms the existing conditions. The liberation of not having to design, detail, and build the exterior enclosure, of accepting an existing volume, structure and fenestration, is critical to the process as well as to the strategy of contrapuntal intervention.

Unlike the design of new buildings, where one controls and consolidates all the critical elements of the building process from the very inception of the project, the design of apartments involves negotiating the inherent constraints of existing conditions—whether plan configuration, ceiling height, orientation, views, window openings, structure, mechanical systems, plumbing or code restrictions. These constraints, rather than being limitations, afford the opportunity for a different type of invention and innovation.

Mies Van der Rohe's Barcelona Pavilion—a horizontal, spatial composition of opaque, translucent and transparent planes "floating" between a grid of steel columns—confirmed the "free plan" precedent and transcended all preconceptions of decorative elaboration. It clarified the essentialness of an edited and integrated material palette.

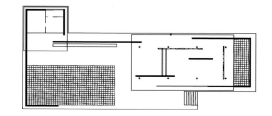

Frank Lloyd Wright's integration of cabinetwork, lighting, and furniture as an architectonic elaboration provided an additional and alternative precedent. In its density, complexity and spatial definition, the composite cabinet/furniture strategy, as we reinterpret it, results in the creation of autonomous objects that can be read as miniature buildings.

The seventeen projects presented in this volume are similar in their implicit obligation to invent and take risks. They represent a variety of formal explorations, each on its own terms summarizing a commitment to a holistic ideology as well as to the idea of singularity. Through a process of self-editing and maturation, the later investigations—beginning with my own apartment and culminating with the Central Park South Apartment—are consistently uncompromising and present a spatial, sculptural, and material clarity that reinforces the initial, referential inspiration—the Villa Savoye.

Paul Goldberger

Introduction

It is unusual for architects of great talent to do some of their best work inside other people's buildings, but Charles Gwathmey is an exception, and not because he is too reserved or too well-mannered to want to make the kind of mark that a determined, ego-driven architect feels compelled to make. He can rev up his ego to the level of the best of them. But Gwathmey's greatest gifts are for the manipulation of space in what we might call a high-resolution, fine-grained way—with intricacy and exactitude—and for the crafting of details and the expression of materials. He and his longtime partner, Robert Siegel, are to their peers as a Swiss watchmaker is to Timex, architects whose gifts lay in precision crafting at small scale. Gwathmey is not, I think, as intellectually engaged by the issues of civic scale as he is by those of private scale—I suspect that he understands the issues of urban design as a citizen but does not put them at the head of his priorities as an artist.

Offer Gwathmey private scale, and he puts more architecture into it than you ever imagined it could contain. That is his genius—he can force architecture into a small box and bring out of it a staggering degree of intensity, which is why he is so often at home working in apartment buildings, especially those in his beloved New York City. It is someone else's box, with a series of constraints that are daunting, and which Gwathmey takes to like a chess master. How to make the space appear to soar when the ceilings are only eight feet high? How to make it flow when there are columns every twelve feet? How to deal with plumbing chases, elevator halls, fire stairs, terraces, windows, and so on—he seems to delight in proving that he can surmount all of these challenges and produce an uncompromised version of his aesthetic. Not the least of the appeal of the restrictions inherent in an existing apartment building, I suspect, is that they serve to remind his clients, many of whom are accustomed to believing that they have the right to build themselves anything they want, that there are still certain limits. It is hard to argue for limits when you are building a freestanding house with an enormous budget; it is easier to accept them in an apartment renovation, and in any case it is much harder for the client to accuse the architect of making them up.

Russell Sturgis once described a particular piece of nineteenth-century architecture as "a box with a pretty inside, put into another box with a pretty outside," the implication being that there was little direct connection between the interior and the exterior. Is this the case with Gwathmey apartments, which often look so radically different from the classical apartment buildings into which they have been inserted? Well, yes, sort of. But not entirely. The stylistic differences are obvious, since Gwathmey has never chosen to move far away from the Corbusian modernism with which he began his career, and virtually all of the apartments Gwathmey and Siegel have designed could be described as modern insertions into more traditional buildings. (The most notable exception is the "roof house" in Columbus, Ohio, a penthouse apartment constructed atop a dreary residential tower. Here, the extravagance of the new space Gwathmey crafted at the top of the building is in counterpoint to the conventional commercial modernism of the building itself.) But these apartments are far more than simply modernist interventions. What is much more interesting, really, is the way in which Gwathmey designs not in opposition to the original architecture, but in subtle accord with it.

In most of these apartments, Gwathmey actually takes his major design cues from what is there. He almost always respects original floor plans, and while he will open up walls and make rooms flow into one another in a way that they are unlikely to have done before, when he is done the living room will probably end up where the original living room was, the kitchen where the kitchen was, and the bedrooms where the bedrooms were. Yet Gwathmey manages to transform these traditional assemblages of rooms into places that are very much his own, coaxing a kind of architectural emotion, even intensity, out of buildings and original apartments that are often genteel, not to say bland. That in itself is striking, since we are accustomed to thinking of modernism as cerebral and lacking in emotion, and of looking to traditional architecture for emotion. Gwathmey reverses this, and shows us that modernism can provide a level of sensuousness beyond what classicism, or at least Park Avenue apartment classicism, is capable of.

Most of Gwathmey Siegel's apartments can be described as sumptuous, even opulent, not to mention as full of feeling. It is not, however, an easy emotion; it simmers beneath the surface of Gwathmey's strongly expressed geometries, but it has the power of a volcano. It is Gwathmey's great skill to be able to channel the volcano's power, never letting it erupt, but always making sure that it permeates the work. There are a lot of words that can describe what he does here, but what captures it best, I think, is to speak of it as passion married to discipline. Passion alone is incoherent; discipline alone is lifeless, but passion and discipline together make art, and their combination is what gives these apartments their soul.

Whether it is the rigorous and disciplined Steel loft or the intricate jewelbox of the Fifth Avenue apartment or the extravaganza of the apartment built in a former gymnasium in the Beaux-Arts police building downtown, every one of these projects begins with a theoretical idea, but its heart, if one can use that term, lies in the experiential. Gwathmey celebrates light, and texture, and movement; he explores mass and proportion, and he is interested in space most of all. I think it is fair to say that in many of the houses and larger buildings, the elevations are less interesting than the spatial configurations and the details (although many of the early houses, with their elevations an expression of their crisp, taut volumes, are exceptions). But even his finest freestanding houses are more interesting within than without, since it is in the interrelationships between internal spaces and in the crafting of small-scale details that his passion lies. Given that, it is no surprise, really, that he does not feel limited by the challenge of designing an apartment. By its very nature, an apartment interior emphasizes those aspects of architecture that Gwathmey takes to most naturally, with no need to deal with the ones that he doesn't.

This book begins, appropriately enough, with the Dunaway apartment [1] in the El Dorado, where Gwathmey's Corbusian beginnings met Emery Roth's Art Moderne fantasies. It is a blunt, self-assured project, with the determination of Gwathmey's famous house and studio for his parents in Amagansett, but not the inventiveness. One senses that at this early point in his career—it was finished in 1970, when he was 32— Gwathmey was less interested in an architectural dialogue with Roth than in obliterating most traces of the original architecture. He wanted to wrestle with an old building, and he proved he could do it.

Unlike his houses, where larger budgets and richer programs did not always yield stronger architecture, the apartments seemed only to get better as time went on, and clients sought more elaborately crafted interiors that gave Gwathmey the opportunity to refine his aesthetic. With the New York apartment, completed three years after Dunaway, one can begin to see where Gwathmey is going. The cabinetry is more elaborate (although not nearly as elaborate as it would eventually become) and it plays a major role in defining spatial relationships. The New York apartment [2] is crisp and clean, like Dunaway, but there is a softness here that is absent in the earlier apartment that prefigures the sensuousness that would emerge more fully in projects like the first Swid apartment, the Geffen apartment, and the Arango and Spielberg apartments, and would be enhanced still more in the second Swid apartment and Gwathmey's own apartment. In these last three works Gwathmey's architecture becomes more intricate, more concerned with grids and patterns as well as with luxurious materials, and there are attempts to create abstract versions of such traditional architectural elements as gateways, rotundas, and panelled walls.

Every so often there is a tendency to gild the lily—the enclosure crafted around the grand piano in the Spielberg apartment, the wooden grille set over the metal grille of a Sub-Zero refrigerator in another apartment —but these come off more as an excess of zeal than as anything else. The Fifth Avenue apartment and the Central Park South apartment, for example, while different in scale, are both ornate, exquisitely crafted objects that contain vast numbers of objects within them, placed with precision within layers of richly textured space. These apartments are a long way from Dunaway, and yet there is the same sense of rigor, the same sense of clarity of space above all, and the same sense that nothing about the design has been done casually.

More and more in recent years, however, Gwathmey has been his own best editor, and there is a sense of a purity and a wholeness in several of the newer apartment projects that manages to combine the richness of the work from the eighties and nineties with the directness and clarity of the earlier work. The Central Park West apartment, for example, while it lacks any particularly new elements, also suggests that Gwathmey had begun by 2000 to break away from what we might call his modern baroque phase that included the Fifth Avenue and Central Park South apartments, and to a limited extent his own. But the finest of these recent works, surely, are the loft Gwathmey completed in 2002 for his stepson, Eric Steel [3], and the huge apartment overlooking Central Park South finished in 2003. In the loft Gwathmey knew enough not to produce too much architecture, and the restraint, in part, is what gives this design its power. The loft is at once controlled and extravagant, like all of Gwathmey's best work; it is awash in light, and it has a profound sense of order that never appears limiting or rigid. Indeed, it is a comforting order, not controlling; as in Mies's finest work, the precision of this design is liberating rather than confining, a rhythm against which human life is played out. The geometries have the effect of making us feel like a natural counterpoint to the architectural forms, and it is uplifting. This is as serene a design as Gwathmey has produced. It deserves a place on the short list of distinguished pieces of architecture that architects have produced for themselves and their families—a list on which Gwathmey's house for his parents, of course, figures prominently.

The Central Park South apartment [4] surely represents a culmination of the work that began more than three decades before in the Dunaway apartment. Like Dunaway, the design is in an older building facing Central Park. Although the new apartment is far larger, the real difference between the two is in the perfection of detail, the sensuousness, and the almost reverential relationship of Gwathmey's architecture to the extraordinary art collection of the owners. From the front door, Gwathmey has directed the eye toward large-scale paintings by Franz Kline and Cy Twombly and a full-size figure by Giacometti, subtly easing the stunning view of Central Park into the background. The textures here are somewhat different from some of the earlier apartments—there is much more metal—and the palette of colors is pale and somewhat silvery, in contrast to the deeper tones of many of the paneled apartments. The use of metal, sometimes textured, sometimes just brushed, makes this very much an apartment of its moment. It reflects the sensibilities of late modernism, although Gwathmey makes them very much his own, and ties them closely to all of his earlier work. It is impossible to be in this apartment and not think of Gwathmey's fundamentally tectonic view of architecture—it is materials and the way they are put together that he loves most of all, and here he has worked with new materials in a way that builds on all of his previous work, naturally and selfconsciously. The real theme here is continuity and evolution.

The original space is not as extravagant here as in many of the apartments, since the ceilings were low and the rooms, in their former configuration, were small. Gwathmey has opened it all up and even pushed up the ceiling in the main living room to create a series of low, gentle vaults, a kind of undulating plane that gives this space distinction without actually making it higher. The reality of this space is horizontal, not vertical, and Gwathmey never fights that—in fact, he pulls you along and through the space so that you always want to look forward, across vistas, down halls, and through rooms. There is always light, and there are always views, even at one point across an airshaft from the back wing of the apartment through to the rooms in the front. Here, surely, is Charles Gwathmey's dream realized—the making of a realm at once totally new and entirely connected to the city, at once a piece of architecture on its own terms, and a part of something else. The rooms flow, one into the next, crisp and relaxed, joining together to make a world of majesterial modernity floating over Central Park.

On the twentieth floor of a 1930s Central Park West building, this space combines two apartments, creating a horizontal volume that slices through the base of the tower, releasing to views on three sides—east to Central Park, south to the Manhattan skyline, and west to the New Jersey Palisades. These extensive views and low ceilings provoked the widening of all major window openings.

One enters a gallery, which opens to the living/dining space and views beyond. Off the gallery is the guest room, library, maid's room, kitchen, and bar/hi-fi room, all of which are distributed linearly front-to-back. Off the living/dining space, articulated by the curved extension of the gallery wall, is the master-bedroom suite, which includes a dressing room, extensive bathroom, and terrace. This space, separated by a mirrored sliding door, is meant to be a literal as well as an illusory extension of the main space.

The edited palette—black slate floor, white walls and ceilings, and black and white lacquer cabinetwork—intensifies the abstract reading of the space.

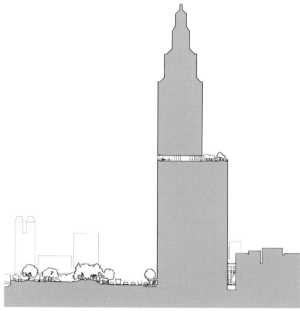

Dunaway Apartment

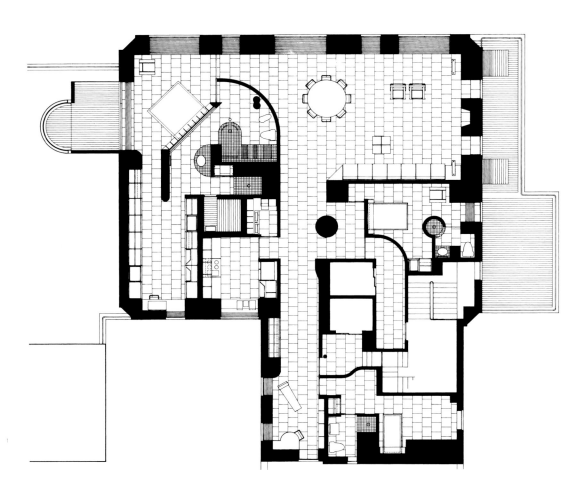

Master bedroom | Master bath

With one window facing Fifth Avenue and the remainder of the space oriented north to buildings across the street, the apartment was divided into two defined zones, living and service, that are connected by a link that could not be enlarged.

In addition to a living/dining space, eat-in kitchen, master-bedroom suite, and a private guest room, the program stipulated separate studies for the writer couple, storage for an extensive book collection, and exhibition space for an important African sculpture collection.

The parti was similar to Whig Hall at Princeton in that the existing frame was modulated by the intervention of a complex new "object" that accommodates both studies as well as the master bathroom and dressing room, while articulating the dining, living, gallery, and book storage spaces. The kitchen and guest bedroom occupy the service zone.

The use of glass block, oak cabinetwork, interior clerestory windows, and sliding mirror pocket-doors, reinforce the transformation of a horizontal, cellular interior into a complex, dual-scaled pavilion that serves as house, office, and gallery.

New York Apartment

Entry gallery

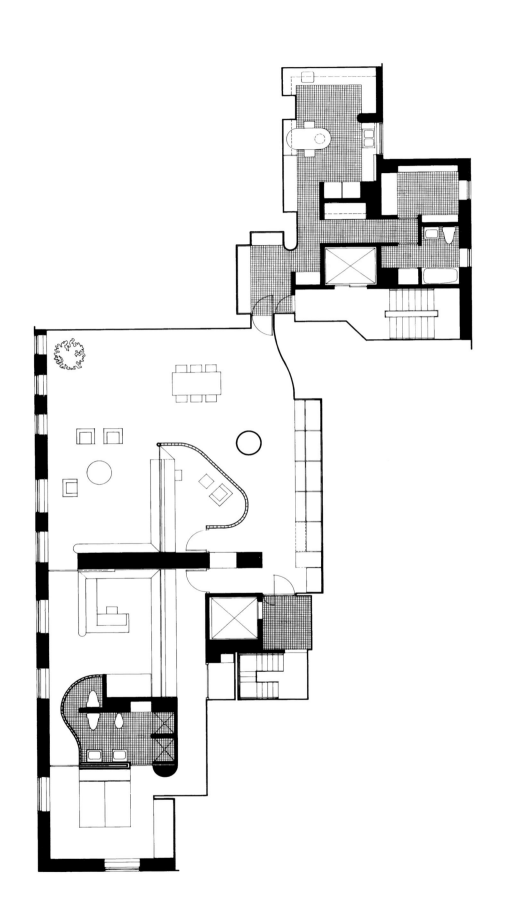

Unger Apartment

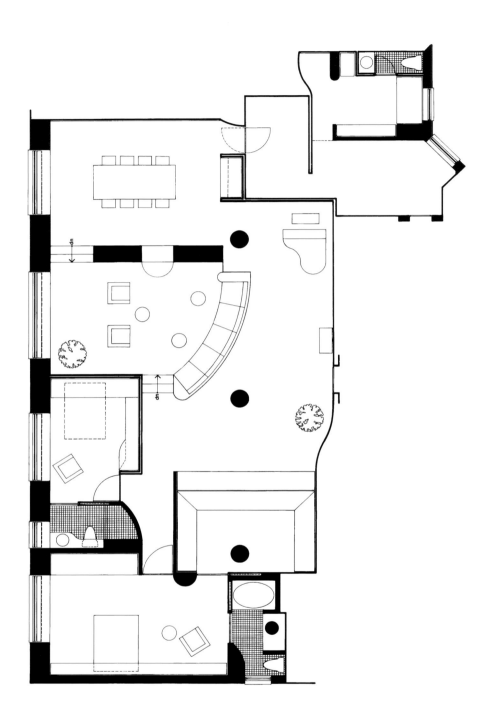

Entry gallery toward living and dining (previous pages) | *Plan*

The client, a fashion designer who entertained and occasionally worked at home, required a large living room, a dining room, kitchen, master bedroom/dressing room, guest bedroom, study, and studio/work space.

The solution was generated by exploiting a fixed fireplace wall and the existing stepped-down living room, typical of the 1940s apartment genre. The living room is defined by a curved built-in sofa that negotiates the step down from the open entry gallery and reinforces the change in section. The dining room, on the opposite side of the chimney wall, reconfigured as an abstract travertine sculpture, connects to both the gallery space and living room.

Swid Apartment I

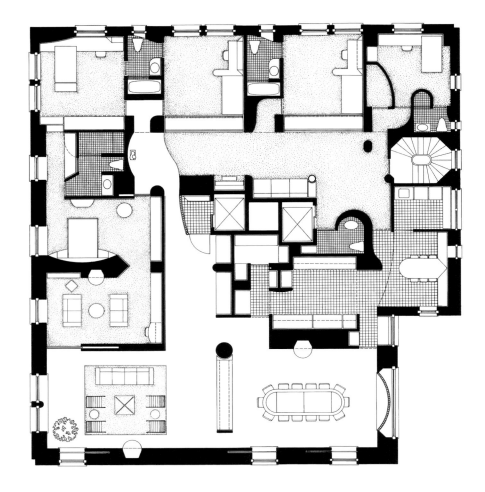

This 3,400-square-foot apartment in a 1930s building was designed to accommodate a couple with three children. The program stipulated a large space for extensive entertaining and the display of contemporary art.

A binuclear plan, anchored by the entry gallery, created two zones—public and private. The living/dining space, separated by a floating cabinet, extends the gallery to the south. The widened circulation space/playroom extends the entry to the north and accesses the master bedroom and library suite, the three children's rooms, the kitchen, the breakfast room, and staff bedrooms.

Changes in ceiling height, variations in floor materials, built-in cabinetwork, and the use of color and mirrors, add a complexity and sense of spatial transformation that was an elaboration of previous explorations.

Living (previous pages) | **Dining from entry gallery**

Family room toward entry and master bedroom

Master bedroom | Family room toward master bedroom

Geffen Apartment

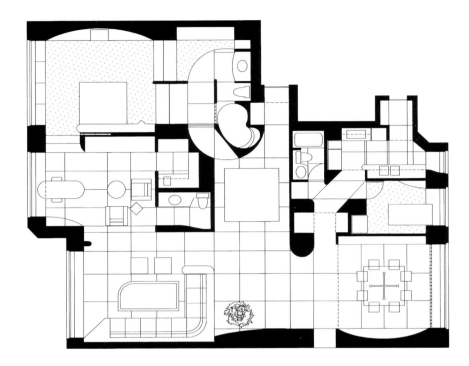

This 1,700-square-foot apartment, with panoramic views west to Central Park and the Manhattan skyline, was reconceived as a continuous volume with an extended sense of space.

The entry gallery widens into a cross-axial living/ dining space and continues around a service core to the study/sitting room. This space, in turn, connects to a master bedroom suite, the floor of which is raised to create a subtle change in section and alter the view perception of the Park. The window wall of the living room, study, and bedroom is rendered in stainless steel, mirror, and lacquered cabinetwork, and integrates lighting, blinds, and heating elements in a referential, ambiguously reflective plane. The kitchen and service areas are in a separate zone off the dining space.

The floor in every room, except the master bedroom, is verte antique marble, the walls and ceilings are painted canvas over plaster, and the cabinetwork is white oak. The composite integration of materials, colors, and textures, and the spatial modulations create a sense of subtle elegance and richness while maintaining the abstract clarity and rigor of the earlier projects.

Master bedroom entry | Detail of master bath | Master bedroom   *Entry gallery toward master bedroom*

The parti for this apartment was anchored by the opening of what became the dining/sitting space into a balcony overviewing the living room, six feet below. This transformation created a volumetrically complex, open public room where, previously, there had been a sequence of small-scale, cellular spaces.

This public room, comprising entry gallery, dining/ sitting, and living, is modulated by a new black slate stair, dark-gray lacquer cabinets, and a single round column. These elements, along with the art, all act as primary objects within the oak-paneled frame.

The perimeter wall, which reinforces perceptual unity throughout the apartment, is deeply recessed, with articulated oak columns integrating the black slate sills and the dropped heads with stepped capitals. The design reaffirms the possibility of a dialogue between abstraction and traditional architectural language.

Arango Apartment

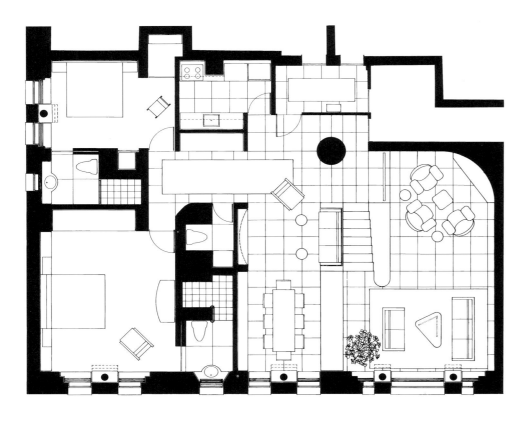

Living (previous pages) | *Master bedroom*

Spielberg Apartment

View from dining   *Living*

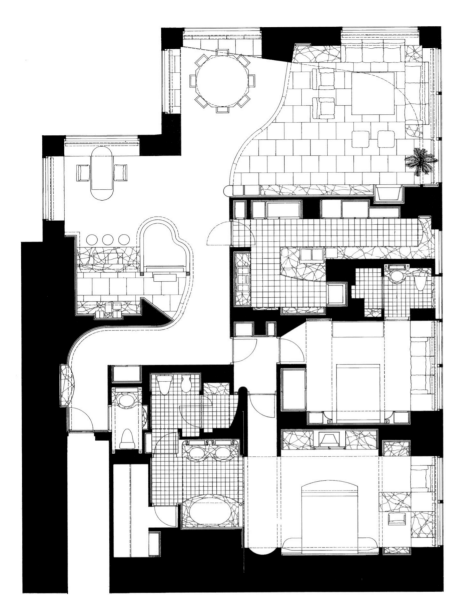

This 2,500-square-foot apartment is located on the fifty-second floor of a prominent midtown tower with spectacular views of Central Park and the city. An autonomous pavilion was created within the existing low-ceilinged, horizontal space by establishing a new envelope detached and distinct from the existing perimeter. This spatial intervention is accomplished by the insertion of usable poché—built-in cabinets and furniture—and reinforced by layers of wood frames and curtains on the window walls, which create multiple planes of transparency, translucency, and opacity along the perimeter.

The spatial sequence is a continuous unfolding of interconnected public spaces from the entry gallery—bar/study, kitchen and living/dining. The private domain, consisting of two bedroom suites, is located off the entry gallery to the east and distinguished by the introduction of local symmetry.

The materials in this apartment—oak and marble floors, ash paneling and cabinetwork, oak doors and trim, and plaster ceiling—are deployed in a system of layers, in both plan and section. This apartment explores the enriched palette, initiated in Geffen, as a further articulation of spatial coding.

Living/dining toward bar

This was our first renovation of a previously designed apartment. The thrust was to accommodate a different and very specific collection of Secessionist furniture that was overlaid on the existing contemporary art collection. The basic plan remained intact, but the materiality and color palette were subtly adjusted to present a perceptually refined environment. The apartment became subtler, and more monochromatic. The architecture became less primary, acting more as a background to the furniture and artwork. Revisiting this apartment allowed us to evaluate an earlier period of work and refine it in response to a new and more specific set of issues.

The primary new element—an abstracted portico, engaging two existing columns—marks the transition from the entry gallery to the living/dining space.

Swid Apartment II

Entry gallery toward living

Entry gallery from living

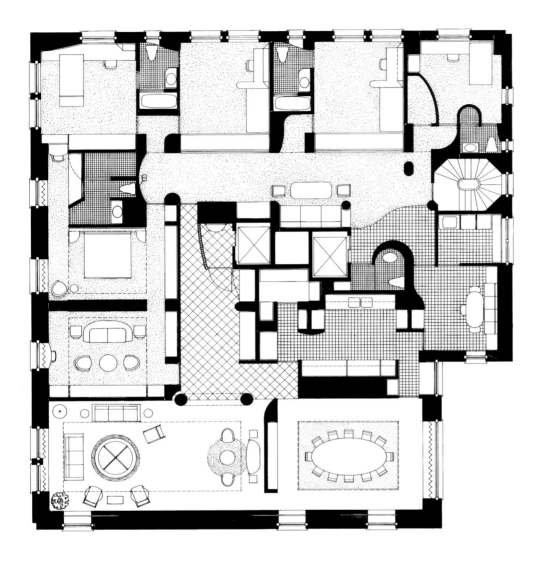

Master bedroom

This was an opportunity, since I was the client, to reject earlier precedents and investigate new ideas without third party constraints. The transformation of this typical, 2,500-square-foot, Fifth Avenue apartment into a spatially complex pavilion, marks the first time that the notions of axial rotation and object/frame are simultaneous and uniform, both in terms of the space making and object placement.

The balance between stable and dynamic spaces is expressed by asymmetrical plan and sectional manipulations that counterpoint yet reengage the orthogonal exterior window walls. The space appears to have been carved rather than assembled, juxtaposing a sense of density with openness and light.

Architect-designed objects, collected over time, allude to historical design preferences and serve as reference points in the object/space dynamic of the parti. The material palette reinforces the programmatic and volumetric manipulation, adding to the sense of collage while supporting the hierarchical articulation of details.

This apartment is both a summary of discoveries made in earlier projects and a speculation on new ideas. It represents a watershed moment in this sequence of investigations.

Gwathmey Apartment

Entry gallery

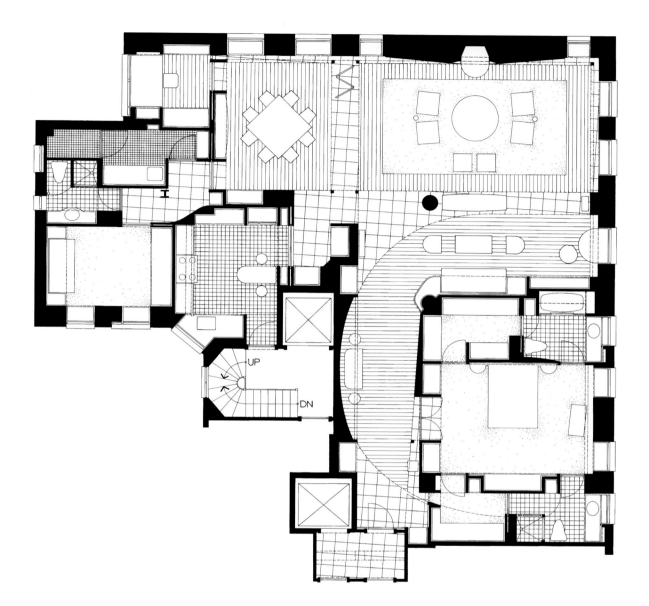

UP

DN

Master bedroom

Master bedroom | *Master bath*

This apartment, designed simultaneously with my apartment, represents a singular notion of container. It is the culmination of that previous sequence of apartments—where the primariness of the orthogonal grid was unequivocal.

The programmatic mandate to evoke an English club, made wood-paneling obligatory. The paneling, a modern reinterpretation, strongly influenced by the Secessionist period, establishes the primary materiality and graphic for the apartment. Space and object are simultaneous and interchangeable, mutually reinforcing, and dense.

A perceptual and literal layering of space is created by the "carving from a solid to a void" and defined by the articulated, inlaid, and modulated steamed beech and cherry wood paneling. The spaces are at once similar yet varied, dense yet open, articulate yet calm.

The "skylit/laylight" gallery is the referential, defining space, connecting and accessing, visually and literally, all the spaces in the apartment. It represents the transformation of "hall," hierarchical and modulated over its length by the varying intersections and transitions.

This apartment was a unique design opportunity which resulted in a resolution that we would otherwise never have come to without the client's mandate. It was provocative and inventive.

Koppelman/Sobel Apartment

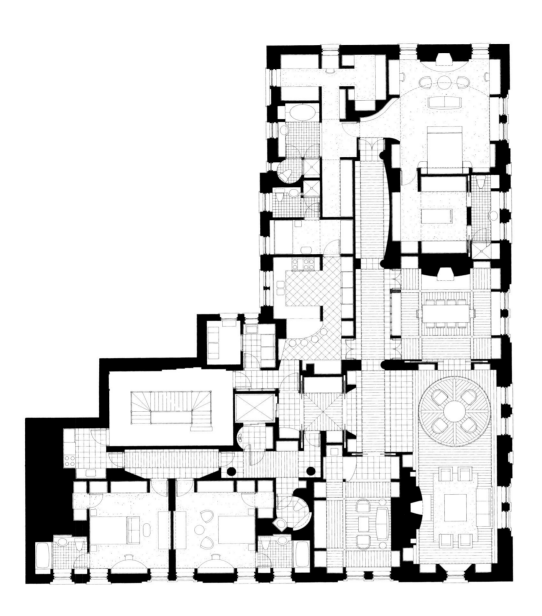

Master bedroom

This apartment represents the transformation of a traditional 1930s, 2,800-square-foot Manhattan apartment—with its attendant program of living room, formal dining area, eat-in kitchen, study, library, master bedroom suite with two dressing rooms, and bathrooms—into a spatially complex modern loft.

The parti is established by three exposed, round columns that support the existing, expressed, beamed ceiling, acting as a "parasol" over the new plan and section. The grid of the limestone floor is rotated from the existing orthogonal plan. Cabinet and bathroom walls are also rotated to reflect this shift. The cabinets that enclose the study and the dressing rooms "float" below the ceiling with glass panels above ensuring privacy while maintaining a sense of openness.

The undulating fireplace wall, articulating the transition from living to dining, is both traditional, treated as a central feature in the apartment, and modern, in its manipulation of the wall plane.

Materials—including limestone, maple, and carpeted floors; integrally colored veneer plaster and back-painted glass walls; and pear-wood and stainless steel cabinets with granite, limestone and onyx tops—are neutral and act as backdrop for spatial interplay.

The asymmetrical manipulations within this apartment express and amplify the dynamic spatial tensions that exist between the frame of the original structure and the modern intervention.

Park Avenue Apartment

Detail of entry hall   *Elevator entry hall*

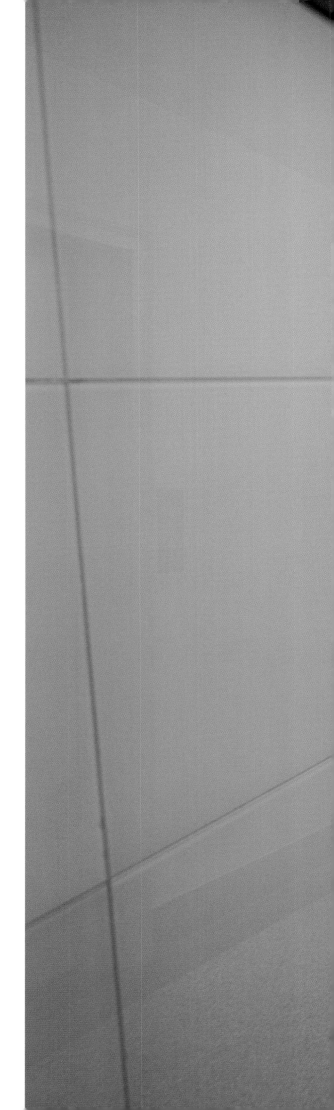

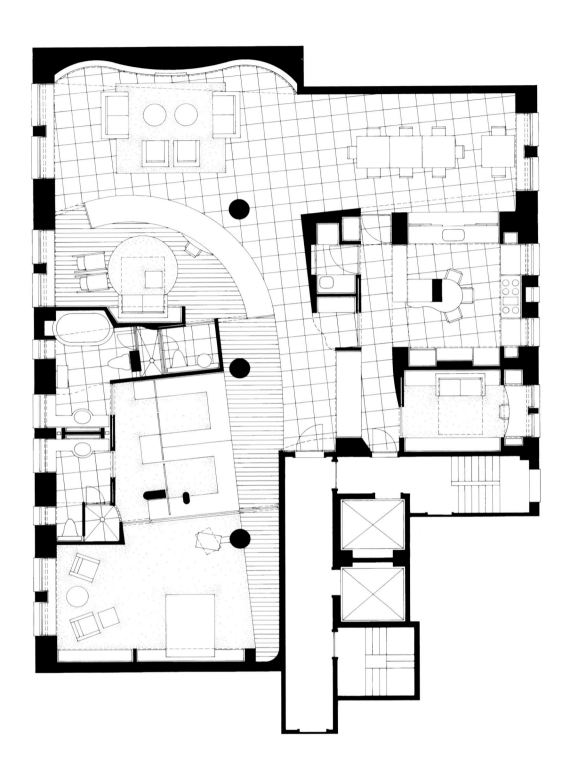

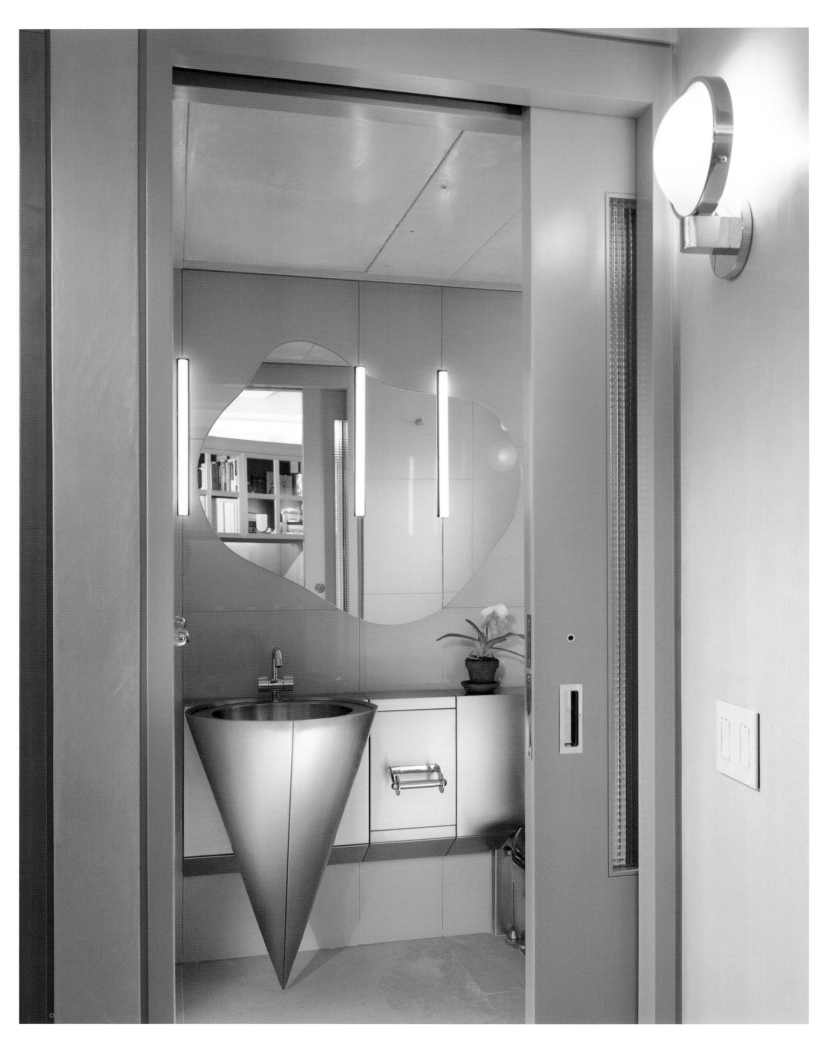

This 2,000-square-foot apartment is located in one of New York's venerable residential hotels at the southeast corner of Central Park.

The architectural transformation was accomplished by reconfiguring the space to exploit the views, creating a vista from the front door to a window looking north over the park. The living/dining space is conceived as a pavilion that is mediated by the intervention of a white glass cube, containing the study/guest bedroom.

The gridded, wood-paneled, east wall of the entry gallery defines the space and accesses the master bedroom suite and kitchen/breakfast "nook."

The material palette of grey sandstone, cherry and maple floors, steamed beech and cherry cabinetwork and paneling, stainless steel, white and patterned glass, and integral plaster walls and ceilings, provides a rich reference for a twentieth-century art and furniture collection.

Fifth Avenue Apartment

Entry gallery

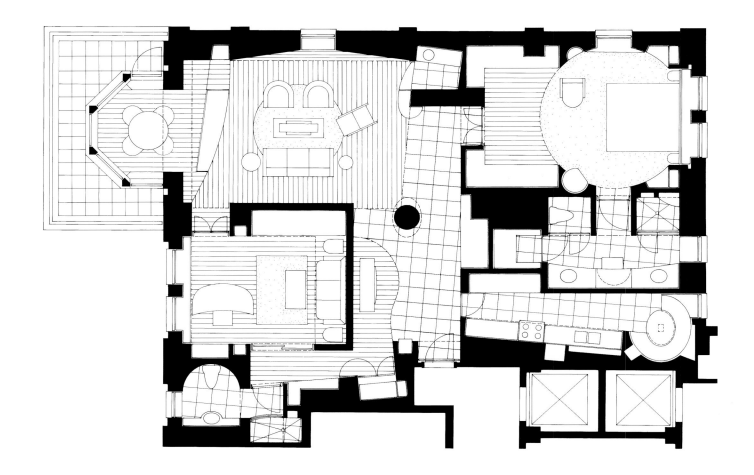

Master bath

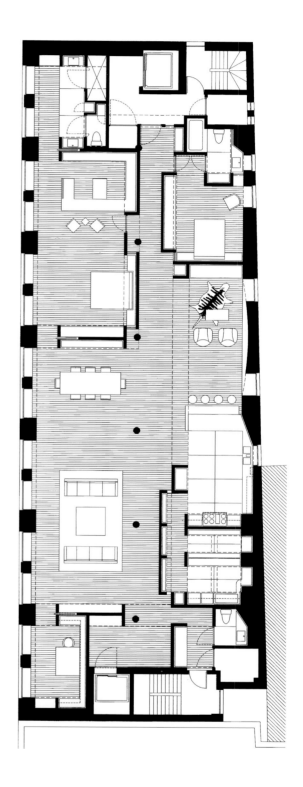

The goal with this apartment was to perceive the "idea" of a single, 4,400-square-foot, rectilinear volume that is hierarchically modulated and articulated through the layering, horizontally and vertically, of the forms and space. The space, 110 feet long by 40 feet wide, has fourteen (seven pair) of south facing windows on the seventh floor of a loft building in Chelsea.

A line of existing columns, eighteen feet from the south façade, articulates the main circulation gallery. A second circulation zone, visual and actual, parallel to and along the south window wall, accesses more private spaces—study, master bedroom suite and master bath—through a sequence of thick wall niches that accommodate sliding steel and patterned glass doors.

The ceiling height to the underside of the slab is 9'10." Existing beams form a second ceiling layer and are the primary referential horizontal graphic through the entire space. Three ceiling/wall heights below the beams establish datums for primary and secondary walls that do not engage the ceiling but float below, exaggerating the illusion of a higher space. These varying ceiling heights afford opportunities to conceal ambient indirect lighting, as well as air-conditioning ducts and grilles, and preserve the overall spatial continuity.

The loft is a three-dimensional reinterpretation of a Mondrian painting; it is an architecture that is at once articulate, graphic, and sublime. It is a space conceived as an "excavation," a carving away that results in an essentialness that is inherently sculptural—light filled, dense and sequential, where nothing is added or redundant.

Steel Loft

Master bedroom

Study toward living/dining

EINSTEIN'S
1912 MANUSCRIPT
ON THE
SPECIAL THEORY
OF RELATIVITY

Gallery toward entry

Detail of gallery

Gallery toward entry

The 3,800-square-foot duplex apartment in the iconic Beresford Building on Central Park West represents a total transformation of the traditional typology. The resulting environment is a spatially dynamic volume that fulfills the formal object/frame strategy through a complex and composite layering.

The primary frame is rendered in integral plaster. Private spaces are defined in wood and separated from the ceiling plane by glass clerestory transoms that reinforce the overall spatial continuity while allowing for countrapuntal, hierarchical intervention and programmatic specificity.

Dining/entry/living form a volumetrically complex, continuous public space modulated by material and level changes that articulate the transition between zones. Integrated furniture and cabinet work further the dual reading of integration and articulation.

The material palette—stone, dark-stained oak, and carpeted floors, stainless steel and titanium, anegré wood paneling and cabinetwork—reinforces the spatial hierarchy and complexity, and establishes a sense of density and permanence.

Central Park West Apartment

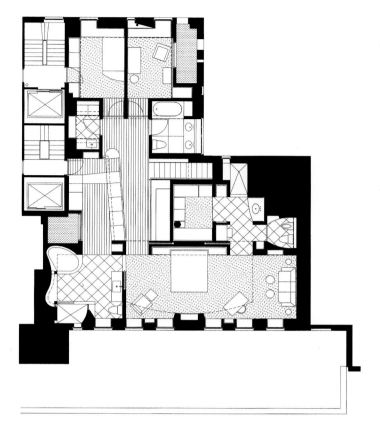

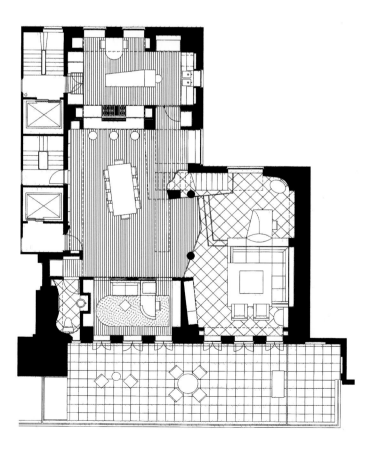

Singers and Standards

NON DIMENTICAR

NATALIE COLE

UNFORGETTABLE, WITH LOVE

ELEKTRA

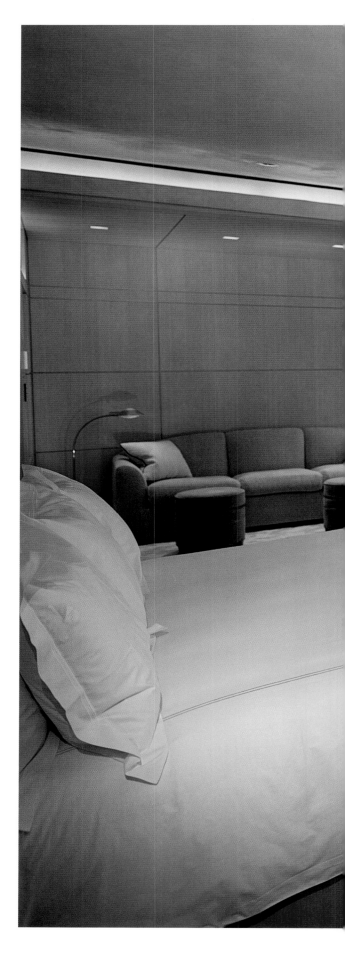

This 6,000-square-foot apartment is located in the former gymnasium of the original Beaux Arts New York City Police Headquarters Building.

The intention was to physically maintain and visually exploit the volumetric integrity and structural expression of the existing barrel-vaulted space, while adding a master bedroom suite and study/library balcony, and integrating an eclectic painting and sculpture collection.

On the main level of the twenty-five-foot-high, steel-trussed volume, is the multi-use living/dining/entertainment/gallery articulated by custom-designed, space-defining furniture. At the east end of the space is the master bedroom suite and study/library balcony accessed by an exposed stair, which rotates at the landing and runs parallel, behind the existing longitudinal steel truss, to attic guest bedrooms over the kitchen, master baths, and dressing rooms.

The study/library balcony is suspended under the east end of the barrel vault and revealed from the master bedroom below, by a continuous radial skylight in the floor, articulating its separation while maintaining the volumetric extension.

The floor of the balcony defines the bedroom ceiling, floating asymmetrically within the existing orthogonal building frame, reinforcing its objectness and sectional variation.

Three large skylights were inserted into the south side of the barrel-vaulted roof, allowing natural light into the longitudinal internal façade of the space and revealing the "classic" building pediment above.

Gymnasium Apartment

Sitting toward study balcony

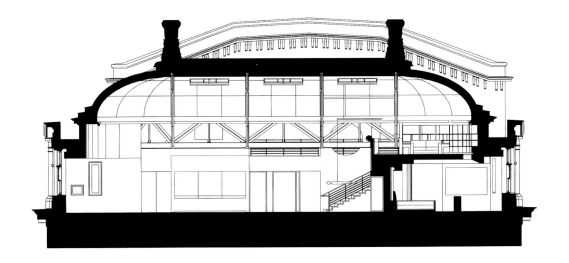

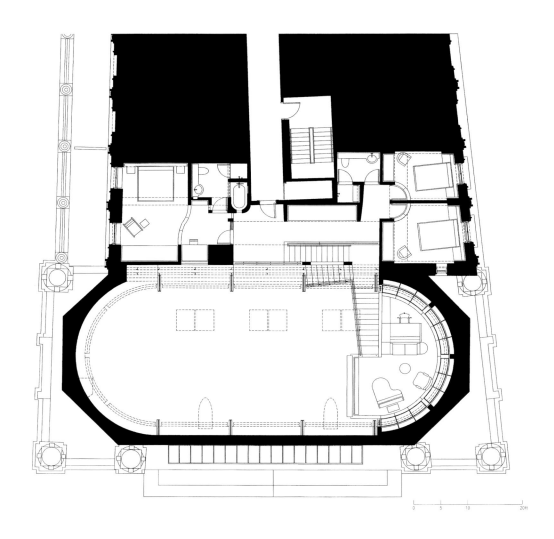

Longitudinal section | Upper-level plan

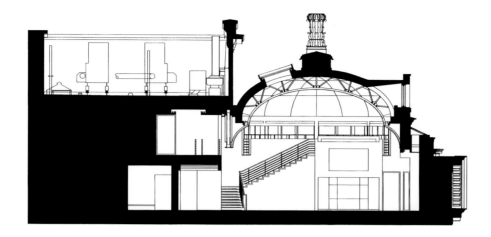

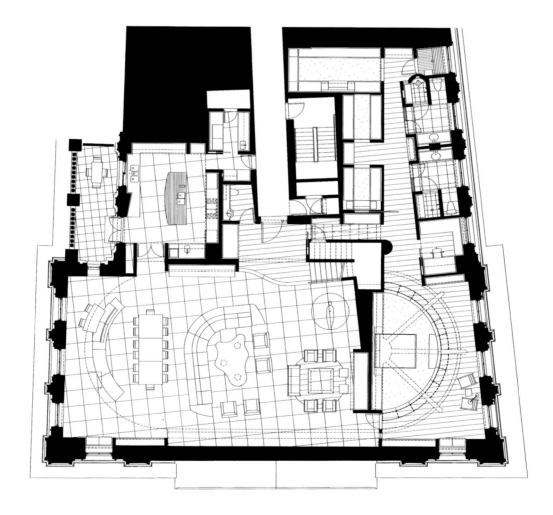

Guest bedroom

Guest bedroom

Miranova Penthouse

The original client request was to renovate the top two floors of a new apartment building in downtown Columbus. Instead, we suggested building a "house on the roof," a new volume that would be specific to the scale of the art collection and program, and that would make an iconic "living top" to a building that had previously been defined simply by a mechanical penthouse.

The entry level is organized around a modulating circulation/gallery space that separates the double-height living volumes, with their views, from the service spaces and building cores.

A 100-foot-long, wedge-shaped, triangular skylight, traversing two-thirds of the plan, releases the roof to the sky and floods the interior with natural light, balancing the two-story-high glass perimeter walls, and adding a dynamic, referential, iconic form to the space.

The program specified a library and private office suite, living space, formal dining space, kitchen/dining/family room, exercise space and spa, master bedroom suite, three guest bedroom suites, sculpture terrace, and gallery.

The entry gallery, accessed from the north elevator lobby adjacent to the two-bedroom guest pavilion, opens to the sculpture terrace and extends the circulation procession to the family spaces that are revealed sequentially.

The second level, accessed by two stairs, one from the main living space and the other from the family room, accommodates the master bedroom suite, with its balcony terrace overlooking the city and river, and a guest bedroom suite, with a balcony sitting area over the library.

The counterpoint between wall and glass, solid and void, establishes a dynamic and hierarchal layering of space that is simultaneously enriched and reinforced by the integration of the art collection into the architecture.

Roof 'house' (previous pages) | *Miranova Building*

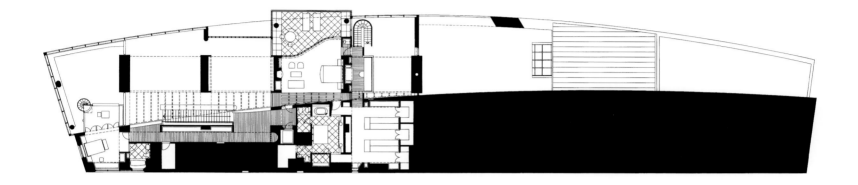

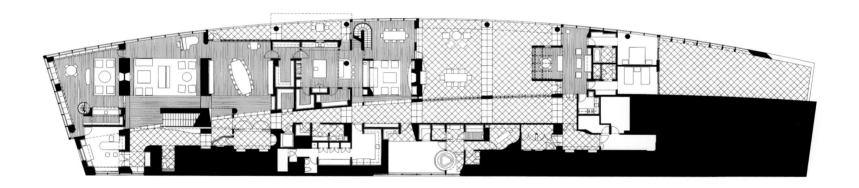

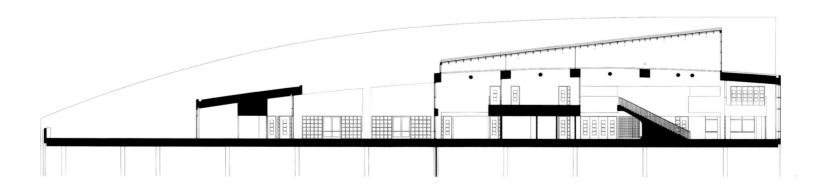

Master bedroom

Central Park South Apartment

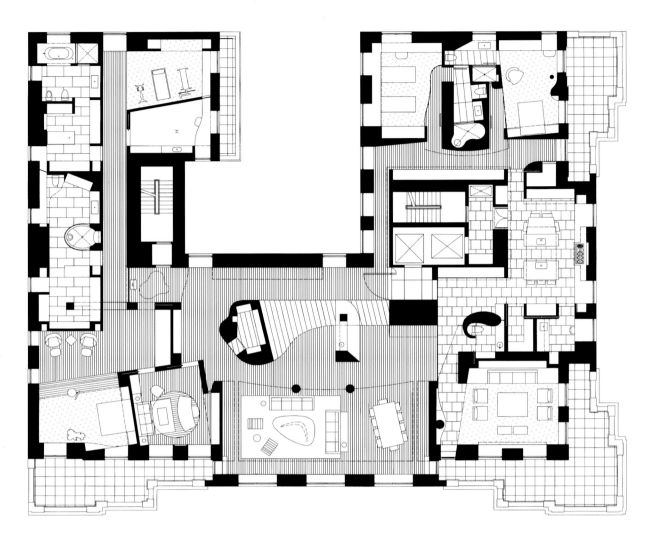

This apartment was designed within an 8,000-square-foot single floor of a hotel building facing Central Park. The existing conditions included ceiling heights of under 8'4" and a random matrix of columns and plumbing lines. The owner, a collector of modern and contemporary art, specified a dense program overlaid with the integration of his art.

On a certain level, this apartment is the consummate summary—a totally sculptural and architecturally articulate series of interconnected spaces with a major view orientation, in this case north to Central Park, which integrates the art with the architecture so that the simultaneity and the dialogue reinforce one and the other.

The extended material palette, referencing a Cubist collage—wood, stone, integral plaster, stainless steel, and titanium—is integrated into a spatial hierarchy that is both subtle and refined. This apartment takes the enriched palette and the sculpted space and, despite all the asymmetries,

results in an incredibly enriched and serene environment. The extended sectional modulation reinforces the sense of variation and disengages one from the perception of being in a low, horizontal environment.

The Gwathmey (p. 100), Park Avenue (p. 124), and Steel (p. 158) apartments are the three investigations that began the development of this density and compositeness, that appears neither restrictive or rigorously imposing.

The architecture is the coequal frame for the art, the furniture, and the view. Every form, every manipulation, and every carving is responsive to either the display of the art, the occupation of the objects, or the reference of the view.

When the space is empty, devoid of furniture or art, it is spectacular in its own right—an environmental sculpture. Everything that was added is an enrichment.

Living/entry gallery (first previous pages) | *Living/dining (second previous pages)* | *Detail of living*

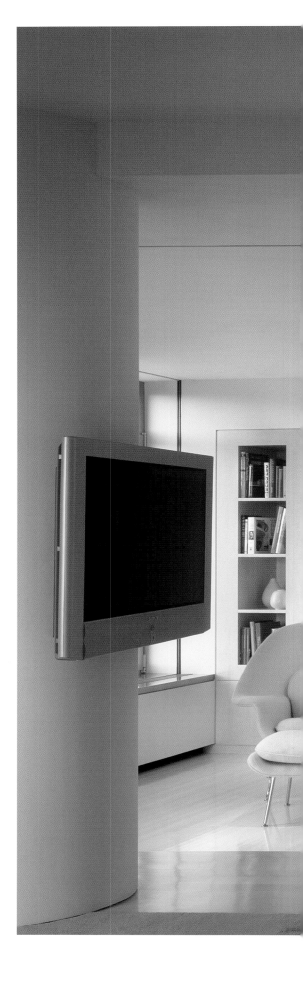

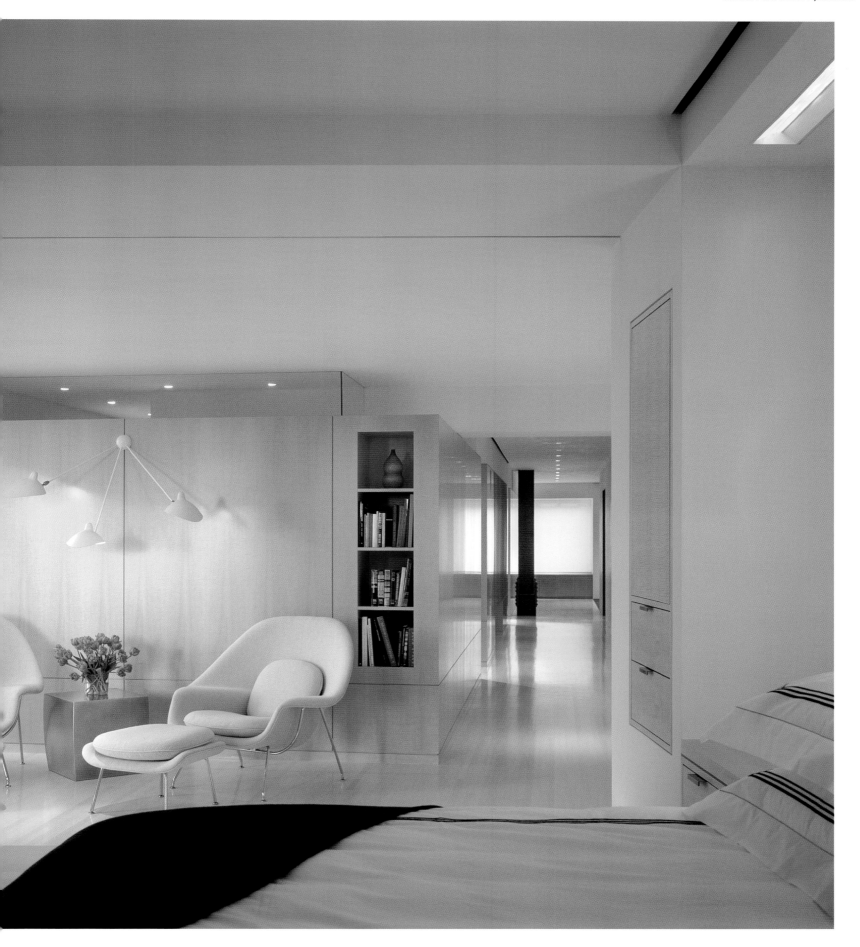

Master bedroom gallery | Studio   Detail of gallery

Bath/dressing (previous pages) | *Bath/dressing*

Gallery toward family room/dining

Detail of family room toward gallery

Gallery toward powder room/kitchen

Kitchen from gallery

Guest bedroom from gallery | *Guest bath*   *Guest bedroom gallery*

Project Chronology

Dunaway Apartment 1969
NEW YORK, NEW YORK

James Swan, Thomas Pritchard, Timothy Wood

pp. 12-21

1981 **Arango Apartment**
NEW YORK, NEW YORK

Jose Coriano, Frank Lupo

pp. 66-77

New York Apartment 1971
NEW YORK, NEW YORK

Timothy Wood, Stephen Potters

pp. 22-31

1983 **Spielberg Apartment**
NEW YORK, NEW YORK

Jose Coriano, Reese Owens

pp. 78-89

Unger Apartment 1975
NEW YORK, NEW YORK

Peter Szilagyi, Gustav Rosenlof,
Tsun-Kin Tam

pp. 32-41

1983 **Swid Apartment II**
NEW YORK, NEW YORK

Jose Coriano

pp. 90-99

Swid Apartment I 1976
NEW YORK, NEW YORK

Peter Szilagyi, Jose Coriano,
Margaret Jann

pp. 42-53

1988 **Gwathmey Apartment**
NEW YORK, NEW YORK

Tsun-Kin Tam, Paul Aferiat, Joseph Ruocco

pp. 100-111

Geffen Apartment 1977
NEW YORK, NEW YORK

Jose Coriano

pp. 54-65

1989 **Koppelman/Sobel Apartment**
NEW YORK, NEW YORK

Dirk Kramer, Lilla Smith, Jorge Castillo,
Greg Epstein, Anthony Iovino, Karen Renick

pp. 112-123

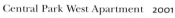

Photography Credits

all other photography courtesy of Gwathmey Siegel & Associates Architects llc.

Richard Bryant/arcaid.co.uk

Spielberg Apartment
All photographs

© **Brad Feinknopf**

Miranova Penthouse
Photograph on p. 220

© **Scott Frances/Esto**

Central Park South Apartment
All photographs

Miranova Penthouse
All photographs except p. 220

Norman McGrath

Arango Apartment
All photographs

Geffen Apartment
All photographs

Swid I Apartment
All photographs

© **Michael Moran**

Park Avenue Apartment
Photograph on p. 143

© **J.D. Merryweather**

Preface
Photograph on p. 6

Durston Saylor

Koppelman/Sobel Apartment
Photograph on p. 112

Edouard Sicot (for *Elle Decor*)

Gwathmey Apartment
Photograph on pp. 102 and 108

Ezra Stoller ©**Esto**

Dunaway Apartment
All photographs

Paul Warchol

Fifth Avenue Apartment
All photographs

Gwathmey Apartment
All photographs except pp. 102 and 108

Gymnasium Apartment
All photographs

Koppelman/Sobel Apartment
All photographs except p. 112

Park Avenue Apartment
All photographs except p. 143

Swid Apartment II
All photographs

Steel Loft
All photographs

Christopher Weil

Central Park West Apartment
All photographs

Tom Yee

New York Apartment
All photographs

Unger Apartment
All photographs